Simple Academic Overview:
Scientific Management

Dr. Jenice Armstead

Simple Academic Overview:
Scientific Management

6" x 9" (15.24 x 22.86 cm)
Black & White on Cream paper
30 pages
ISBN-13: 978-1484844984 (CreateSpace-Assigned)
ISBN-10: 148484498X
BISAC: Business & Economics / Management Science

Disclaimer

The reader should use their own judgment in utilizing the information in this book. The reader should seek advice from professionals as needed. The author's advice and information are based on professional experiences The author/publisher shall have neither responsibility nor liability to any person or entity with respect to any damages directly or indirectly as an aspect by any advice or information contained herein.

Dedication

This book and series is dedicated to knowledge hungry students, academic knowledge workers, educators and motivators of the business and business related fields.

Continue to Empower Others,
Dr. Jenice Armstead

Photo Credit: Davina McGinnis

TABLE OF CONTENTS

Biography

Dr. Jenice Armstead is a military veteran, author, motivational speaker, Professor and Academic Business Department Chair with over 17 years professional experience in the public and private sector. Jenice's expertise covers human resources, business management, the federal hiring process and government hiring policy. She understands the significance of human capital value for organizational development. She has an exceptional aptitude for teaching difficult topics with practical approaches. Jenice has a MBA with a Concentration in Human Resources from Saint Leo University and a Doctorate of Business Administration from Jones International University.

Forward

Foundations of Management Science

This book provides an historical overview of the development of management principles during the Scientific Management Era. Including key scholars, principles, and insights, as well as notable critiques of scientific management. Human resources managers today, explain principles of scientific management as the topics are related to organizational policy, organizational development and also promote organizational growth.

Introduction

The scientific management era began during World War II, in the United States and spread abroad which allowed organizations to implement necessary changes to businesses practices along with developing usable management practices for organizations. The United States Government set laws and policies in place, and proclaimed scientific management principles into the industrial workforce. With the economy at an all time down fall, scientific management examined business progression and focused on evolution of policy development with an emphasis on workforce improvement and performance management productivity. Industrial and labor relations took the lead in keeping in greater profession where management often was represented. The scientific management era outlined the need for developing operational policies, determining business objectives and goals for creating a stronger workforce.

Scientific Management Era

Scientific management historically gives relevance to the industrial era by precisely outlining ambivalence to the jurisdiction of shifting management thoughts to new ways of analyzing business practices. The scientific management era of thought is more than implementing policies and regulations; it gives understanding of the importance of human capital as a key business relation. There was a need to strive for the highest degree of productivity for not only the employee, but for the organization as a whole. In order for organizations to be productive, scientific management era developed organizational policy and structures to assist with organizational development by improving the competitive edge of a business. The principles of the scientific management era ascertained environmental uncertainty for businesses. The newly developed principles allowed for organizations to influence positive changes for organizational structure.

Scientific Management Era: Key Scholars, Principles, and Insights

The Father of Scientific Management, Fredrick W. Taylor, revolutionized the workforce by greatly influencing the scientific management era and changing business management thought of the workplace. Taylor's achievements in scientific management effectively educated business owners by revealing the "business influence" based on principles from "The Course of American Democratic Thought." Taylor discusses scientific management and business development for organizational profitability (Rowlinson, 1988).

The thought behind the scientific management era was to turn out a higher quality of work, but the catch was businesses had to pay employees more. The principles increase competitiveness, and allows for organizations to stay current in an ever-changing business market (Freedman, 1950).

Organizational structure is everything. Take for example fast food chains; they work much like the scientific management era functioned. Each fast food chain has an exact business structure for how food is prepared, how long it should take for the customer to receive their food and the quality of their food being served to customers. The fast food industry competition is stiff, and a "meal deals" are a dime a dozen, the key is to ensure the prices are low enough to still be competitive to keep the customer coming back. This is where scientific management comes in the picture. Scientific management is objective, it allows for numerous business methods to be analyzed and evaluated based on the benefits as they relate to what "works" and what "doesn't work" for the organization. This is the reason why some fast food companies have survived, and competitors have conquered others.

Organizational Policy

As a human resource professional, implementing an organizational policy of "science of work" is one of the scientific management approaches that give a fresh management thought to "old ways" of doing things. When an employee is motivated to work using a positive method verses a negative method, the employee results will be different. Using the "science of work" takes the management compensation principle, and changes the focus to the employee. For example, organizational structures, which base compensation on, hours worked are a standardized way for employees to understand how their wages are earned. But, if an employee has options for compensation other than working a set amount of hours, the results are more favorable. "Teleworking" is an excellent way to motivate employees to work; while working from home is not an option for all organizations it is an employee benefit when implementing "science of work" into organizational policy. If an organization implemented an organizational policy of "Teleworking" for employees to work, the amount of hours worked would not seem as stressful for the employee. By supplying employee's options to take care of personal items while using a "Teleworking" schedule as an alternative to coming into work everyday, this works as a motivational tool. Implementing new organizational policy is a win-win for the entire organization, along with keeping moral high. Scientific management evolves a vast array of aspects such as using "Teleworking" schedules to focus on organizational development.

Training and development is another benefit to the organizational policy implementation. Training and development of employees gives employees a sense of belonging. When employees feel they are apart of an organization, their work performance will increase. Training and development empowers employees to grow professionally, and strengthens the employee/management relationship by showing the employee their value in the organization. Training and development ensures all efforts from the organization are directed toward a common goal of promoting excellence for the employee. In order for an organization to acquire a healthy structured foundation, employee value needs to be substantiated. Businesses have the ability to grow and gradually develop training programs with using techniques such as computer-based training. The key concept in implementation of any training and development program involves communication with employees. With the policy development focused on employee value, organizations secure their longevity among their competitors.

Conclusion

Understanding the importance of implementing scientific management principles pertains to organizational policy development, implementation and step-by-step follow through. There are many ways to implement changes that consist of low difficulty levels for employees to adjust quickly to the changes. In all fairness, scientific management is highly objective, organizational policy starts with businesses laying the foundation for how employees will be expected to preform.

Truth be told, the "scientific management" approach is a natural part of management, which can be oversimplified if not developed and implemented correctly (Freedman, 1950). The implemented methods give indicating factors of problems, along with grounding ways to solve those problems. Management's understanding of problems within the business gives the business an immediate competitive edge over peer businesses.

References

Freedman, H. (1950). Scientific management in small business. *Harvard Business Review, 28*(3), 33-53.

Rowlinson, M. (1988). The early application of scientific management by cadbury. *Business History, 30*(4), 377-395.